Terror To The End

The Last Day in the Life of Charles Dickens in His Own Words (More or Less)

BY JAMES R. ZIMMERMAN

iUniverse, Inc.
Bloomington

Terror To The End
The Last Day in the Life of Charles Dickens in His Own Words
(More or Less)

iUniverse books may be ordered through booksellers or by contacting:

iUniverse
1663 Liberty Drive
Bloomington, IN 47403
www.iuniverse.com
1-800-Authors (1-800-288-4677)

A Plumpies Press Production

ISBN: 978-1-4620-8299-5 (sc)
ISBN: 978-1-4620-8300-8 (ebk)

Printed in the United States of America

iUniverse rev. date: 12/21/2011

INTRODUCTION

*C*harles Dickens died on June 9, 1870 after suffering a stroke the day before, when he had reached the halfway point of his final and unfinished novel, *The Mystery of Edwin Drood*. Dickens had prematurely left the stage during his "Farewell Tour," thus abruptly ending a performing career that included nearly 500 extraordinary one-man shows. Still, despite several doctors' orders, Dickens had been recently seen performing the most demanding of his "readings" out loud to himself at his home, Gads Hill, on the Gravesend Road, between London and Rochester. But why does any of this matter to me—or possibly, to you?

I believe it's obvious: we are imaginative beings, and we are naturally curious about the humans whose imaginations have been most productive. They are exactly like us, but somehow they have expressed their nature in a way that shows us our own. When we read and re-read many works by the same author, we often come to say that we "love" the author. In practice, for many affectionate and attentive readers, this results in an accumulation of biographical facts and favorite anecdotes. Sometimes the author becomes, in effect, a character in the reader's own real-life adventure.

For me, this has long been the case with Charles John Huffam Dickens. I was captured by the creations of the desire-ridden, suffering man whose sacrifices and duty-bound consciousness drove him to excesses of restless accomplishment. As I age, I continue to travel through life with The Great Inimitable as a cheerful if sometimes manic sidekick. In other words, the long-dead Dickens has terminally captured my poor imagination, and I am, in some way, a creature of his. Not that other authors, poets, painters, playwrights, and film directors haven't had an enormous impact on me. But, in most cases, they, too, have confessed to the debt owed to Dickens. To me, in practical terms, Dickens eclipsed Shakespeare as a cultural force—but only because, in his own work, Dickens knew (and exploited) Shakespeare so thoroughly.

I suppose, as a child, I was vaguely cognizant of Scrooge as most American children are made to be in one way or another, but I didn't distinguish what I knew of Dickens' Ebeneezer Scrooge from what I knew of, say, Walt Disney's Scrooge McDuck until, back in The States after spending a year in another former British colony (the then fifteen-year-old Republic of India), I was assigned to read an abridged version of *Great Expectations*. After that adolescent experience, a mixture of fantasy and mystery, it was only a matter of time before I managed to read everything by what came to be "my favorite author."

From the designation of favorite to the involvement with the biography, my interest in Dickens "the man," or Dickens "the person," or Dickens "the rock star" continued to grow. Eventually, in my mind, we became fellow characters in the grand sweep of history. I frequently referred my own trials, errors, tribulations, and triumphs to his. When Dickens was forty years of age, I would think, what was he doing?

So Dickens began to haunt me. Dickens loved the notion of ghosts. And all the relations between the living and the living, and between the living and the dead seem to go on changing over the years. As Stephen Dedalus says in *Ulysses* about Dickens' beloved Shakespeare and that great artist's memorable creations and legacy, a ghost is . . .

> One who has faded into impalpability through death, through absence, through change in manners. Elizabethan London lay as far from Stratford as corrupt Paris lies from virgin Dublin. (154)

How far does Dickens' London lie from us. How far did it lie from Gads Hill as he was dying? Unimaginable distances are at play here. *Terror to the End* is a bold attempt to obliterate the unimaginable and bring Dickens into the room where we read. Only the reader's imagination can make that happen, finally—and that imagination is aided by the reader's knowledge of and affection for the long-dead man.

I have studied Dickens under Richard D. Altick, who was kind enough to approve of a recorded version of an earlier script. I have seen performers like Bert Hornbeck trying to bring Dickens to life for Americans. But no stretch is greater than the remarkable effort Dickens himself made when he killed Nancy on the stage. In fact, he was killing himself.

When I was in my fortieth year, in 1989, I went to Gads Hill Place, centrally situated in geographical, historical, and, for us in the twenty-first century, practically mythological terms in the midst of Great Literature, including significance in the literary realms of both Chaucer and Shakespeare. I got a brief tour of the interior, explored the tunnel, smiled at a pair of friendly magpies, and then had a pint or two at the Sir John Falstaff across the Gravesend Road. Later, I drove into the marshes and stopped at the church with not nine but thirteen lozenges. I had already begun to compose the present piece, and I had an actor in mind, the brilliant Claywood Sempliner, whose career I had happily followed from Ann Arbor to New Orleans to New York.

Now I have outlived the great man, and I have no further fun in asking what he would be doing at my age, so I've resorted to other amusements in relation to him. If any of this makes even the slightest sense to you, and you haven't yet enjoyed the superb Dickens resources on offer, I suggest that you read Edgar Johnson, Philip Collins, Frederick Busch, Fred Kaplan, and the Pilgrim collections of his letters.

If you just want to ruminate over the possible activities and reflections of Dickens prior to his fatal stroke, and you're willing to suspend your disbelief with me for awhile, you may enjoy some of what follows. I confess that I project backwards wherever the record of the man's statements and writings leaves me wondering; I fantasize a boy who blossomed in the uncertainties and contingencies familiar to us, and a man who was one of us—extremely active, inclined toward adopting new attitudes and new technologies, and consumed with creating and interacting and doing more than merely consuming what others offered for purchase. In short, the Dickens I have come to "know" (or imagine) is a "modern" man, and perhaps even a "postmodern" one, if we liberally enlarge the term to include anything and everything. In any case, I readily identify with Dickens' own Mr. George Silverman, who wrote out these lines:

> At length I was presented to a college living in a sequestered place, and there
> I now pen my explanation . . . . I pen it for the relief of my own mind, not
> foreseeing whether or no it will ever have a reader.

Most documents and authorities agree that on June 8, 1870, Charles Dickens finished the sixth of the projected twelve parts of *The Mystery of Edwin Drood*, then suffered a stroke. Or perhaps yet another stroke. One account suggests that he said he wanted "to lie down—on the ground." He had never regained consciousness when he died the next day. By the end of his life, the world-famous novelist was more interested in performing on stage than producing fiction and journalism, and his favorite performance was "Sikes and Nancy," the sensationally brutal murder scene from his early novel, *Oliver Twist*. "Favorite" is too weak a word for the staggeringly ferocious and brutal murder of Nancy; by all accounts, including his own, he couldn't stop performing the scene, even to himself when he was alone, as he purportedly did soon before his fatal stroke. Not that the *Oliver Twist* murder was the only violence in Dickens, of course. You immediately think of Bradley Headstone, that homicidal stalker who all but dominated Dickens' penultimate novel, *Our Mutual Friend*.

In its violence as much as in its insightfulness and sentimentality, this script is conceived as a one-man show to honor "The Readings" performed by Dickens in Great Britain and The United States as well as to celebrate the great personality and larger-than-life character who began writing short fiction as the semi-anonymous "Boz" and ended as an international celebrity whose characters' names and stories had permanently entered global culture and the English language. Nearly five hundred times, the famous novelist transformed himself into a spellbinding stage performer—a one-man show-stopper—working from his own scripts. To call them "readings" is to reduce them by a hundredfold from the power they had over their audiences. Dickens was an unprecedentedly charismatic and even frightening actor. Using his own novels as the basis for his carefully constructed scripts, he memorized the words and mesmerized the audiences—if he didn't virtually murder them!

Violence and power struggles are evident throughout Dickens' life and work: the lawsuits, the Thackeray controversy, and of course the murderers and bad men—

Bradley Headstone and Eugene Wrayburn, Steerforth, Bill Sikes, Scrooge, the villain turned benefactor in *Great Expectations*, and the brutality throughout *The Tale of Two Cities*.

In addition to offering insight into the significance and power of the performances he gave on stage, *Terror to the End* shows the man at work, creating and composing on the penultimate day of his life and his last working day. We see his characters as they come into being and as they will be remembered as long as the generations of the future continue to read (and make motion picture adaptations of novels).

Someday, science fiction may fade away and historical fiction may completely take over the market. The further we get from the time of Dickens, the more the technology and culture looks strange to us—as alien as any science fiction.

These days, we might call the suffering Dickens endured subsequent to the Staplehurst Railway Disaster "post-traumatic stress disorder." Most likely, he also suffered a series of smaller strokes. In any case, he was very unwell, near death, and still fighting to be that extraordinary person who was so much more than a bestselling novelist.

Dickens would die on the day after this imaginary soliloquy, and his wishes (as expressed in the script that follows) would not be honored. In fact, his very public burial would include three days of public mourning, with thousands of fans queuing in the line at Westminster Abbey to get a glimpse of the great man.

The conceit undergirding this project is simple: it's a short step from performing privately (even secretly) to yourself—as he was witnessed having done—to talking to yourself. The text is presented here in a kind of modular form as an invitation to prospective producers and directors to easily customize a script for their own purposes. I urge anyone with any interest at all to try it out as a reading or a casual production. My interest is in the possibility of anything at all coming of this. Invite me—I'll be there if I can. After all, everything we do in this vein is merely an imitation of—and a homage to—The Great Inimitable.

The setting is of course Gads Hill Place, Dickens' country home on the Gravesend Road between London and Rochester. The vibrant but exhausted, distressed, and doomed man has just emerged from his custom-built tunnel under the Gravesend

Road, entered the front door of his house, and strode into his study. A word to the squeamish: portions of what follows are not fit for the faint-hearted. And I sincerely apologize for the bit about the dog, but it was Dickens' doing, not my own.

—JZ, December 13, 2011, Port Republic, Virginia

TERROR TO THE END

[Dickens in his performing voice, as the breathless, sensational narrator of the spine-tingling, homicidal piece, "Sikes and Nancy," or "The Oliver Twist Murder."]

"The housebreaker freed one arm and grasped his pistol. The certainty of immediate detection if he fired, flashed across his mind; and he beat it twice upon the upturned face that almost touched his own."

[Gasps, and then faintly moans.]

Who's there? Georgina, you're not spying on me, I hope? Kate? Mary? Not Dolby, is it?

[Aside.]

I only wish it were my dear Ellen.

[Muttering.]

One of the servants, no doubt, watching me. They all have to watch me. And if they catch me doing "Nancy" again, they will tell me I am not permitted it.

[Fierce.]

Who goes there? I know someone is listening.

[Delighted, gentle.]

Why bless my soul, it's only you, isn't it! You there, in my poor head. To have such a vast public and yet to have to imagine you—that's what I have been reduced to now that I have been forced to break off the Farewell Reading Tour.

Yes, I know I shouldn't do "The Murder." The doctors don't allow it! But here I am in my own house, and no one can stop me! It gives me a respite from my troubles.

Lately, I've been in that wandering . . . unsettled . . . restless . . . uncontrollable state of being about my new book, *The Mystery of Edwin Drood*. The first monthly part sold fifty thousand copies!

Just now, in my little chalet across the road, I very nearly finished the sixth number of the twelve monthly parts that will make up *Edwin Drood*. With a little more work, I can reach the halfway point.

Today I've been working like a dragon!

I am wonderfully clear about my writing for a change, but I don't deny that I have had some trouble over this book. Well, of course, I haven't attempted a novel in five years—since *Our Mutual Friend*. I am a little out of practice, that's all.

I have hopes that I may make a success of *Drood*—if, please God, I live to finish it. I say "if" because, you know, I have not been well lately.

My poor head has so much *not* fiction that *will* be thought of when I don't want to think of it that I am forced to take more care than I once took. I admit I do not see my way as clearly as I once did. I make headway but slowly. And I sometimes feel as if I had read something by somebody else which I should never get out of my head.

I am sometimes a wretched sort of creature in my way, but it is a way that gets on somehow, and all ways have the same finger-post at the head of them, and at every turning in them.

Lately, I have been slow to recover from various difficulties. I have had to limit my usual activities. It was a long and bitter winter—dark and bitter. I can still feel it in my leg, my head, my heart. But I am trying to put all that behind me now. I must finish this number of *Drood*.

Of course, you know I believe in the case of some of my books I must have been even worse!

I would sit down to work, do nothing, get up and walk a dozen miles, come back and sit down next day, again do nothing, go down a railroad, find a place where I resolve to stay a month, come home next morning, go strolling about for hours and hours, reject all engagements, walk about in the country by day, then prowl about in the strangest places in London by night.

I did say to myself sometimes when I am a little impatient, "How can you be such an erratic, wayward, unsettled, capricious, incomprehensible beast? I am ashamed of you!"

It seems my roaming days may be behind me. Not to mention my touring days. Sometimes I think even my writing days are near their end.

But today of all days I have had such a run of it, and I see it so clearly. And, after all, I am only just fifty-eight years of age.

There is absolutely nothing wrong with me! I've always combined my sedentary powers with the active training of a prize-fighter. When the papers say that Mr. Charles Dickens is in a critical state of health it is a misprint for cricketing!

Yes, you see, just thinking of my powers has put me in quite a brilliant condition already. I should be almost ashamed of myself if I didn't know the unconditional knocking off for a time from all reading wear and tear to be a cautionary rather than a curative measure.

Of course, it is not easy dwelling for so long in the mind of a murderer! Oddly, then, to do "The Murder" from *Oliver Twist* is more than mere recreation. It is to fall back into a murder I know so well!

One of the qualities that makes me different from other men is the intense pursuit of any idea that takes possession of me. Sometimes for good, sometimes, I daresay, for evil.

Were it not for my various manias, I might have been a better father and a better man.

But I keep forgetting myself. I have a deadline, just as I have always had.

Just a few hundred words more, and I'll be halfway home. Let's see, where was I?

[Reading his manuscript.]

Ah, yes, here it is. Mr. Datchery goes to bed. So how to get him up again? Let's see. "A brilliant morning." That's it. That will get him up and about!

[Speaking the words as he writes them, with occasional asides.]

"A brilliant morning . . . shines on the old city."

I see Rochester in the bright mornings of my youth.

". . . the old city. Its antiquities . . . and ruins . . . are . . . beautiful."

No, let's make that "surpassingly beautiful."

And so they are. What else?

"With the . . . lusty . . . ivy . . . gleaming . . . in the sun . . . ."

Can you see it as I do?

"And the rich . . . trees . . . waving . . . in the . . . balmy . . . air."

And the light—I have it—like it was this very morning in the chalet!

"Changes of . . . glorious light . . . from moving boughs . . . songs of birds . . . scents from gardens, woods, and fields . . . or rather from . . . the one . . . great garden . . . of the . . . whole . . . cultivated . . . island . . . in its . . . ."

What?

"*Yielding* time!"

There, you see—just like the old days!

I am often asked how I *do* it. It's quite simple, really. Everything is *visible* to me. I see my characters in action before my very eyes.

Sometimes I *become* the character. If necessary, I resort to the looking glass to see myself as him.

So you see my performances in "The Readings" are really nothing new. With one thing and another—not to mention all of the amateur theatricals—I've been acting all my life.

For example, in the case of this chapter, which I have called "The Dawn Again"—I always love to see the dawn—I must imagine myself as Mr. Tope.

[Acting out his invention.]

"Comes . . . Mr. Tope . . . with his large keys . . . and yawningly . . . unlocks . . . and sets open."

You see how I do it? Later, then, Mrs. Tope.

"Comes Mrs. Tope . . . and attendant . . . sweeping . . . sprites . . . ."

"Come . . . in due time . . . organist . . . and bellows boy . . . peeping down . . . from the . . . red curtains . . . in the loft . . . fearlessly . . . flapping dust . . . from books . . . up at that . . . remote . . . elevation . . . whisking it . . . from stocks and pedals."

I can almost imagine *my*self as the Cathedral *it*self!

You see, I can go on and on and on like this. In fact, I must.

"Come . . . sundry . . . rooks . . . from various quarters . . . of the sky . . . back to the great tower . . . who may be presumed . . . to enjoy . . . vibration . . . and to know . . . bell and organ . . . are going to give it to them!"

"Come a very small . . . and straggling . . . congregation . . . indeed."

As you see, I imagine everything. Every detail. Every character, however insignificant, and every scene, no matter how brief.

When I say I imagine them, I do not really think them up. They simply present themselves to me, and I see them.

I see Dick Datchery just now.

"He contemplates . . . a very small score . . . in the old . . . tavern . . . way . . . of keeping scores . . . illegible . . . except to the scorer."

"Hmph! A very small . . . a very poor . . . score."

"He signs . . . over the contemplation . . . of its poverty . . . takes a bit of chalk . . . from one of the cupboard shelves . . . and pauses with it . . . in his hand . . . uncertain . . . what addition to make . . . to the account."

"He speaks to himself . . . ."

"I think . . . a moderate stroke . . . is all I man justified . . . in scoring up."

"So . . . suits the action . . . to the word . . . closes the cupboard . . . and goes to bed."

[Pensive, melancholy.]

Just so. I see it all before me. And yet the curious thing is that I cannot always see myself.

[Lighter, quizzical.]

I myself am quite a difficult subject, as the recent photograph of me quite obviously shows.

I fancy the image is nothing at all like me, as I am. It has a grim and wasted aspect, and perhaps might be made useful as a portrait of "The Ancient Mariner."

[Then, suddenly, all business again.]

But this day advances, and I have not yet completed my chapter. Yes, "The Dawn Again." It soon will be in earnest if I fail to attend to this little business now, while I see everything so clearly.

And it will have been a good day indeed. A little more work here and I shall chalk up a very thick stroke, from the top of the cupboard door to the very bottom, and then I shall fall to my dinner with an appetite!

[Re-reading, in a confident, yet tranquil manner; almost elegiac.]

A brilliant morning shines on the old city. Its antiquities and ruins are surpassingly beautiful. With the lusty ivy gleaming in the sun, and the rich trees waving in the balmy air, changes of glorious light from moving boughs, songs of birds, scents from gardens, woods, and fields—or rather from the one great garden of the whole cultivated island in its yielding time.

You see, I can still do it. How much longer can I do it, that is the question. I shall be content if I can finish *Drood*, which, by the bye, is the first of my books that carries in its contract a clause about . . . my death.

I have to make certain arrangements because, you see, I am not well.

I remember when I used to say that I hadn't so much as a headache in twenty years! But all that has changed.

[Pause; slight shudder.]

It was five years ago tomorrow, on the ninth of June, 1865, when dear Ellen and I were among the unfortunate victims of the Staplehurst Railway Accident.

My favorite watch had palpitations for six months afterwards, and perhaps if I had given it a rest it would have recovered sooner—or more completely.

In fact, I can never be much nearer parting company forever with my public than I was then, until there shall be written against my life those two words with which I have closed every book.

Since the accident, I have been a changed man. And yet I am myself as always, and I still have a positive mania for making improvements in the house, for reading, for roaming, for life!

But I know that my own life is near its end. It's true, and I have had to make certain stipulations so that these things are done in a sensible way.

With all this fuss about my health, my friend Collins—Wilkie Collins, you know, the famous novelist who writes about mystery and death in his detective novels—when Collins is here for one of his frequent visits, and I am across the Gravesend Road writing in the chalet, he will send innocent messages to ask, with his compliments, how I find myself now! When we are in the same room he likes to take my pulse.

Perhaps, he and I might agree, Mr. Charles Dickens should have given a timely rest to his favorite watch five years ago.

[A small, disgusted sound.]

Never mind that now. Today I have been my usual inimitable self!

When I take up my pen, I see my opening perfectly, with one main line on which the story is to turn, and if I don't now strike while the iron—meaning myself—is hot, I shall drift off again, and have to go through this uneasiness once more.

You seem to be a stranger here. Perhaps you haven't yet seen the first number of *Drood*? Shame on you! Well, no matter. Let me tell you a bit about the setting and the story.

"Drowsy Cloisterham." You know right away of course that it is Rochester, where I was a child, and where I have indicated that I wish to be buried.

[Sniffs; clears his throat.]

Here, try this. You'll see how the plot grows entangled in my murder mystery.

[Reading; performing.]

"Drowsy Cloisterham, whenever it awoke to a passing reconsideration of a story above six months old and dismissed by the bench of magistrates was pretty equally divided in opinion whether John Jasper's beloved nephew had been killed by his passionate rival treacherously, or in open struggle . . . ."

Why is it that murder stories seem to press forward into my mind from all sides?

Here I am, now, back in Kent, where my early imaginations dated. I took them away from here so full of innocent construction and guileless belief, and I've brought them back so worn and torn, and so much the worse.

Where was I? I wanted you to hear this: light . . . birdsong . . . scents . . . penetrate into the Cathedral.

It's usually such a dark place. Like a great tomb, really.

"Subdue . . . its . . . earthy . . . odour . . . ." Yes! ". . . and preach . . . the Resurrection . . . and . . . the life."

[Pause; sigh.]

That's all very well, but I cannot help thinking that my own life is near its end. It's true, and I have had to make certain stipulations so that these . . . things . . . are done in a sensible way.

I have emphatically directed that they bury me in an inexpensive, unostentatious, and strictly private manner.

Furthermore, I want no public announcement made as to the place or time of my burial.

At the utmost, I should wish not more than three plain mourning coaches be employed—and that those who do attend my funeral wear no scarf, or cloak, or black bow, or long hat-band, or any other such revolting absurdity!

Some will say that I am unkind by these harsh prohibitions, but you know that is not the case.

You, my Public, you my readers, you to whom I have told every one of these stories, you believe, that even with a host of imperfections and shortcomings on my head, that I have as a writer tried to be as true to you as you have been to me. And you have been very true to me indeed.

The Readings have proved this. All I had to do was take a book in my hand and read, at the appointed place and hour, and come out again.

And when I do read, I do not write—I only edit. It is merely an interpretation of myself.

The Readings have taken the place of the amateur theatricals we used to do for private audiences. They are so important to me. (Perhaps now, if I am to believe the doctors, I should say *were*.)

Until I began the Readings, I had no contact with my dear Public, except for the occasional odd encounter—and odd it often was!

I remember the elderly charwoman who attended my eldest child when he was ill. She was of course illiterate, but had once gone to a subscription tea at a snuffshop where the landlord would read each month's number of *Dombey and Son*.

Evidently she was very much impressed by what she heard, for when I came to visit my boy, and this poor old soul found out that I was Charley's father, she said this to the lady of the house, as it was reported to me later:

[CD does the elderly charwoman's voice.]

"Lawk, ma'm! Is the sick young gentleman upstairs the son of the man that put together *Dombey*? Lawk, I thought it must have taken three or four men to put together *Dombey*!"

[CD, reflecting, pleased, proud, and a bit nostalgic.]

The Readings allowed my Public to see me as I am—and for me to be there in the same room with them. I knew they would take immensely—I first thought of the idea years ago—and of course there is much money to be made in this sort of thing, although some may see it as a bit *infra dig.*

Of course, I meant to be an actor upon the stage when I was young and in love, but that is quite another, and quite a sad, story. Or perhaps it is, at this remove, rather a comic story, as I made it out to be with poor Flora Finching in *Little Dorrit.*

Much later, when I first seriously entered on this sort of interpretation of myself, I was sustained by the hope that I could drop into some hearts some new expression of the meaning of my books that would touch the Public in a new way.

Of course, it was natural to begin with something from *A Christmas Carol* and *The Cricket on the Hearth.* That sort of thing. And that was all very well. I had no idea of murdering Nancy on the stage at that time!

I simply meant to show up and read—but I admit that there's nothing in the world equal to seeing the house rise at you, one sea of delightful faces, one hurrah of applause!

I tried to do my best, and many in the audience appreciated my efforts. One man wrote, "Hear Dickens, and die! You will never live to hear anything of its kind so good!"

Hear Dickens, and die, indeed! Be Dickens, and then what?

[Sigh.]

To this very hour, as I struggle with *Drood* and fuss about my failing health, a similar purpose is so strong in me, and so real are my fictions to myself, that, after hundreds of nights before the audiences—and after all that I have endured—I could still come with perfect freshness to that little red table, with my prompt copy waiting there, and laugh and cry with my hearers, as if I had never stood there before!

But when I think of reading again, I do not think of Scrooge and Tiny Tim, or Bardell and Pickwick, or Mrs. Gamp, or even my dear David Copperfield and his friend Steerforth.

When I think of reading again, I always think of doing "Sikes and Nancy," the murder scene from *Oliver Twist*.

When I first thought of doing the murder of Nancy, I wanted to leave behind the recollection of something very passionate and dramatic, done with simple means, if the art would justify the theme. I dare say it did.

In any case, I worked up "The Murder" and began trying it alone by myself—as I still like to do—but I found that I had got something so horrible out of it that I was afraid to try it on the Public!

That was seven years ago. Then, just two years ago, when I had decided upon "The Farewell Tour," I was tempted to finally do "The Murder" on stage.

But I was still unsure. So much so, that I mounted a trial performance with one hundred very special guests in the audience.

When I did "The Murder" for them, all of my guests turned unmistakably pale, and had horror-struck faces!

My reverend friend William Harkness said afterward that he had an almost irresistible impulse upon him to scream, and that if anyone else had done so, he was sure to have followed.

And that great ladies doctor Priestly warned me about doing "The Murder" in public:

[Dickens does the doctor's professional, confidential, and slightly pompous voice.]

"My dear Dickens, you may rely upon it that if one woman cries out when you murder the girl, there will be a contagion of hysteria all over the place!"

And the famous actress, Mrs. Keely—when I asked her, "What do you say—do it or not?"—said:

[Dickens does a histrionic female voice.]

"Why, of course! Do it! Having got such an effect as that, it must be done! But . . ."

And here, she rolled her large black eyes very slowly, and spoke very distinctly:

". . . the Public have been looking for a sensation these last fifty years or so, and, by Heaven, they have got it!"

And then there was Macready—the greatest actor in the history of the theater, the supreme Shakespearean, manager of Covent Garden and Drury Lane theaters—Macready, whom I first saw as a mere boy, when I was one of his most faithful and devoted adherents in the pit. And as I improved myself, in mind and fortune, I only became the more earnest in my study of him.

Macready was seventy-five when he saw me do "The Murder." He sat in the front row and stared at me.

Afterwards, in the dressing room, he stared at me some more. I tried to laugh him out of it, but he would not be laughed out of it.

He was old, and ill, and slow, but he summoned strength enough to declare:

[Dickens imitates the long-retired, very emotional old actor.]

"No Dickens! Er . . . I will not . . ."

He paused, and I did not know whether he would continue. And then, with sudden emphasis, he said:

"I will not . . . er . . . have it . . . uh . . . put aside! Er . . . in my best times . . . uh . . . you remember them, my dear boy . . . gone! Gone. No . . . ."

And now he paused and seemed to stop, but then began again with even greater emphasis:

"It comes to this, uh . . . two . . . Mac . . . beths!"

After this startling outburst, Macready stood with his glass in his hand, and his old square jaw, his fierce form, looking defiantly at my poor manager Dolby, as if Dolby had contradicted him.

And then, sadly, he trailed into a weak, pale likeness of himself, as if his whole appearance has been some clever optical illusion.

Two Macbeths, indeed!

[CD chuckles, contentedly.]

"The Murder of Nancy" seems to transform everybody. Why, when I perform it, I don't think a hand ever moves, or an eye looks away.

Inevitably, there comes a fixed expression of horror of me all over the theater, which could not be surpassed if I were going to be hanged from that red velvet table.

Not that I don't pay a price for these violent delights! For my own part, my pulse gets high, and my doctors make me lie down during Intermission, then argue among themselves whether or not I should be allowed to go back out again.

One night, in the midst of a reading, I couldn't even say, "Mis-ter Pick-wick."

I think I called him "Pickswick," and "Peckswicks," and even "Picnic"—all sorts of names except the right one.

It is the result of some sort of brain mischief.

There seems to be degeneration of some functions of my heart. It does not contract as it should. I have noticed for some time a decided change in my buoyancy and hopefulness.

In other words, in my usual tone.

It all goes back to what they still call "The Staplehurst Disaster."

It wasn't until days after the railway accident that I realized how it affected me.

I suppose I had been something of a hero, rushing about among the wreckage, making sure of Ellen's safety first, of course, and then attending to the scores of others, dying and bleeding and screaming upon the ground.

To this very hour, I have sudden vague rushes of terror, even when riding in a hansom cab, which are perfectly unreasonable, but quite insurmountable.

To see how this distresses me, you have to understand that I used to think nothing of driving a pair of horses habitually through the most crowded parts of London.

I cannot now drive, with comfort to myself, on the country roads here—and I doubt if I could ride at all in a saddle.

Railway traveling, I can no longer bear. I had a perfect conviction, with anything like speed, that the carriage was down on one side—and generally the left, which is not the side on which the accident really went over.

And when the train jolted over the intersections, I held the arms of my chair. My face turned white, and I broke out in perspiration.

It was inexpressibly distressing!

Dolby, my travelling secretary, knew those odd momentary seizures of mine so well that he would instantly produce a dram of brandy, which rallied the heart and generally prevailed.

I still can't bear to be hurried or flurried. Although I feel all right at the moment, even now I suffer from a rather dazed sensation of being greatly fatigued.

I remember thinking not so very long ago that the mere physical effort and change "The Readings" represented would be good as another means of bearing my condition.

And yet "The Readings" have torn me, and I am a broken man.

One reading in particular, you know, is the one that has finally ruined me. It is as if I murder myself when I murder the girl—and kill Bill and his dog.

It was bad judgment, even madness, ever to have given the reading in the first place under the conditions of a traveling life—and worse than madness to give it with such frequency.

I had doctors with me. They said my pulse was seventy-two when I began the reading, but when I had finished it was one hundred and twenty-four!

Imagine! I made the crossing from Ireland in the worst of hard weather, after a very tiring week there, and then I read in London and Cambridge and Norwich.

After that, to Colchester just in time for an early dinner, and the next morning to Swansea betimes, and the next away to Cheltenham, where I read two successive nights, before returning for another London reading, only to start immediately afterwards to Hereford!

When I had to break off "The Farewell Tour," I made sure that a document signed by my doctors was circulated which represented the nature of the case in its true light. I so detested the idea of disappointing you, my loyal Public, that I went to some lengths to have the true situation made clear:

[Dickens assumes what he imagines to be the voice of the doctors' letter.]

"We the undersigned certify that Mr. Charles Dickens has been seriously unwell, through great exhaustion and fatigue of body and mind consequent upon his public readings and long and frequent railway journeys."

You might well ask me, "Why do you wish to lead such a life as this?" "Why do I?" I ask myself, and often have these thirty years!

And what is it that makes me think of poor Nancy just now?

[CD becomes Nancy.]

"I told you before that I was afraid to speak to you here. I don't know why it is . . . [SHUDDER] . . . but I have such a fear and dread upon me that I can hardly stand. Of what I scarcely know. I wish I did. Horrible thoughts of death—and shrouds with blood upon them—and a fear that made me burn as if I was on fire."

[CD is instructive, then reflective.]

Do you see how she senses her own approaching death? Hmm.

[CD is Nancy again.]

"I was reading a book today, to while the time away, and the same things came into the print. I swear I saw 'coffin' written in every page of the book in large black letters!"

[CD recalls his second trip to The United States.]

This reminds me of something. When I was last in America, I learned the story of President Lincoln's death. He knew the fear and dread of death on the very day of his assassination! And to think, it was barely five years ago, so close to the time of my own near death.

How such a man as Lincoln could be slain! The United States is a distracted land of troublesome vagabonds—the most extensive and meanest of scoundrels.

What can you expect from a people who are made up of off-scourings of other countries?

America! I was drawn inexorably to that wretched place—drawn by profits! Just as the Charles of my own creation—Darnay in *A Tale of Two Cities*—is drawn to the Lodestone Rock in France!

Americans have been robbing me for decades with pirated editions of the novels. It was about time I took some money out of America!

Twenty thousand pounds! Why that's more than ten times what I paid for this house!

To get such a sum in a heap so soon was an immense consideration for me. I have my wife's income to pay, a very expensive position to hold, and eight living children to support—six of them boys, and all six with the curse of limpness upon them!

You don't know what it is to look around an enormous dinner table and see reflected from every seat of it some horribly well-remembered expression of inadaptability to anything!

I expect to be presently presented with a smock frock, a pair of leather breeches, and a pewter watch for having brought up the largest family ever known with the smallest disposition to do anything for themselves!

What a wonderful instance of the general inanity of kings, that the kings in the fairy tales should have always been wishing for children! If they had but known when they were well off—having none!

[CD grunts, composes himself.]

Where was I? I meant to tell you something of particular relevance.

Ah, yes, I have it. Of course! President Lincoln's death—and how he dreamt the same dream three times, and told it to his Cabinet the very afternoon of his assassination, these five years ago.

At the last meeting of the Cabinet—and I have this from his Secretary of War personally—the President sat with a special air of dignity, instead of, as Stanton put it to me, his usual manner:

[CD doing Stanton's voice.]

". . . lolling about in the most ungainly attitudes and telling such questionable stories."

[CD in his own voice, again, intensely.]

No, in his last Cabinet meeting, Lincoln was different, with his chin sunk upon his chest. When asked what was the matter, the President revealed a secret.

[CD doing Lincoln.]

"I have had a dream for the third time now—I am on a great, broad, rolling river, and I am in a boat, and I drift, and I drift . . . ."

[CD, dramatically.]

That evening he was shot.

[Pause, clears his throat.]

Like President Lincoln, and like poor Nancy, I have such a fear and dread upon me that I can hardly stand.

Sometimes the most overwhelming feeling comes upon me—and I want to lie down. On the ground.

I have written in the margin of my prompt book for "Sikes and Nancy"—and double-underlined the words—"Terror to the End." And so it is for me, and always shall be, as long as I, please God, am allowed to go on.

[Pause; then a sudden outburst as Nancy.]

"Bill, Bill! For dear God's sake, for your own, for mine, stop before you spill my blood!!! I have been true to you, upon my guilty soul I have!!!"

[CD, exhausted and confessional.]

I cannot help myself. I am Nancy and I am Bill, and I am all of my most unfortunate characters all rolled up in one.

And it has been the ruin of me.

So, you see, it wouldn't do for me to resume the Readings after all, either here or in Australia, where they say, in one quick tour I could make more money than I ever dreamed possible!

Although, in spite of everything, I of course continue to entertain hopes of fulfilling the final schedule of my "Farewell Tour," I know that even that is . . . unlikely.

After what must have been well over five hundred performances, if you count the amateur theatricals I organized with Collins, I have no doubt spoken my final words from the stage, which were these:

[CD doing his histrionic stage voice.]

"From these garish lights, I now vanish forevermore, with a heartfelt, grateful, respectful, affectionate farewell."

[CD, himself, subdued.]

There is always something sad about the last of anything. It is always difficult for me to say goodbye, as if it's bad luck.

[Chuckling.]

And I especially hate to say goodbye to the money the Readings brought in. I feel the absence of it already.

That is why I remained at home this morning and wrote. And I must yet reach the halfway point of *Drood* before I leave off work. But first, let me tell you where I wrote so brilliantly this morning.

I spent my morning in Switzerland! Not literally, of course. I only wish it were so. But I spent my morning in my chalet, a real Swiss chalet in miniature, complete with a balcony on the top level. It was a gift from that great actor, Charles Fechter.

I discovered Fechter myself—in Paris. I remember thinking, "A man who can do this, can do anything!" So I brought him back with me to England to be in one of those pieces Collins and I wrote. Grateful chap, Fechter. He sent me the chalet.

It came in crates. So many of them. Why, I had no idea. The groom said to me:

[Dickens does his groom's country voice.]

"Fifty-eight boxes have come, sir."

[CD as himself.]

"What?" I said, thinking I had not properly understood the man.

[Groom again.]

"The fifty-eight boxes have come, sir. They be piled up outside the gate, sir, and we shall soon see what they are!"

[CD, proudly.]

I have put five mirrors in the chalet and, while I write, they reflect and refract all kinds of ways—the leaves that are quivering at the windows, and the great fields of waving corn, and the sail-dotted river.

My room is up among the branches of the trees, and the birds and butterflies fly in and out, and the green branches shoot in at the open windows, and the lights and shadows of the clouds come and go with the rest of the company.

[Elegiac.]

The scent of flowers—and indeed of everything that is growing for miles and miles—is most delicious.

[Resigned.]

That is my Switzerland for now.

[Pause. Re-thinking.]

To walk across the Alps—can you imagine? No, there is no chance I will be able to really quit England this year.

[Excited.]

And yet I think I could sometimes!

Lord bless you, I feel sometimes that I am going to take up my alpenstock and cross all the passes.

And I am going to Italy, and I am also going up the Nile to the Second Cataract, and I am going to Jerusalem, and to India—and likewise to Australia!

[Pause. Resumes the realistic, ironic, cheerful vein.]

My only dimness of perception in this wise is that I don't just know when I am going. If I did but know when, I should be so wonderfully clear about it all!

[Pause. Mournful.]

No, there is no chance I will be able to quit England this year.

[CD as Narrator of "Sikes and Nancy," starting quietly, and gradually growing in intensity.]

"The Housebreaker freed one arm . . . and grasped his pistol.

"The certainty of immediate detection if he fired flashed across his mind . . . and . . ."

[Violently.]

". . . he beat the pistol twice upon the upturned face that almost touched his own."

[Pathetically.]

"Nancy staggered and fell . . . but, raising herself on her knees, she drew from her bosom a white handkerchief . . . and holding it upwards, toward Heaven, breathed one prayer for mercy to her Maker."

[Brutally.]

"It was a ghastly figure to look upon. The murderer staggered backward to the wall, and, shutting the sight out with his hand, seized a heavy club . . . and struck her down!"

[Catching himself. Remembering his audience.]

Yes, I know. I pace and I rant, and it's not good for me. The doctors would not approve. They may be right. I grant you, I did suffer the strangest nervous miseries until I stopped doing the Readings.

And yet I have rested these many weeks, and sometimes I feel that it has been a year. Unless I am active, there is something in me that is always rusting and corroding me.

Restlessness has always driven me, and I cannot help it. I feel if I can't walk far and fast when I want, I shall explode and perish! Which may be soon!

When I still lived in London, under the same roof as poor Kate, my wife, it was, if possible, worse.

I remember one night, getting up, and getting dressed at Tavistock House, my former home in London, where my wife still resides. I was very much put out by something, no matter what. Perhaps I will explain it presently.

In any case, I walked all the way here, to Gads Hill Place, in the dead of night, a distance of thirty miles.

I am a great walker, or I was, and it has saved me many times, most especially when my domestic unhappiness was so strong upon me.

And yet the memory of that unhappiness remained for so long so strong upon me that I couldn't write sometimes and, when I was walking, couldn't rest one minute.

To have time to myself, to get tired of myself, and yet not to be able to come out of myself to be pleasant to anybody else!

To go on turning the same wheel round and round, and over and over again, until it may begin to roll me towards my end!

[Attempting a lighter note.]

Why, if I could afford it, I would wear a part of my mane away as the lion in The Zoological Garden has done, by rubbing it against the windows of my cage.

I have sometimes felt as if I could have given up, and let the whole battle ride over me. But that has not lasted long, for God knows I have plenty to cheer me in the long run.

[Trying to laugh himself out of it.]

When you think what a game you've been up to ever since you was in your cradle, and what a poor sort of chap you are, and how it's always yesterday with you—or else tomorrow—and never today, that's where it is!

My wretched childhood did have its happy moments, I suppose. My father loved it when, as a child of five, I would sing:

[Dickens imitates himself as a boy of five, singing.]

"Long time I've courted you, miss
And now I've come from sea
We'll make no more ado, miss
But quickly married be!"

[Ironic.]

Pity that I chose to act out that childish air when I was barely an adult!

[Nostalgic.]

My poor father delighted in my comic singing ability. He made certain everyone else did, too, by displaying me on a table top. Yes, he would stand me up on a table in a public place and bid me sing that very song.

We were frequent visitors at a beautiful hotel not far from here—in Rochester, of which I am writing just now, in Drood. Which makes me think, I should be getting back to it.

But stay a moment. I must tell you about my sister Fannie, who was just two years my elder, and the other half of the entertainment. Standing by the table below me, she would answer me back, quite appropriately, I might add:

[In Fannie's childish singing voice.]

"I ne'er will wed a tar, sir
Deceitful as yourself
'Tis very plain you are, sir
A good for nothing elf!"

[Laughs at the recollection; then becomes serious.]

Poor Fannie was always an excellent singer. I was with her shortly before she died these many years ago. Consumption, it was. She had studied at The Royal Academy of Music, but then her poor son came along. My idea for Tiny Tim came from him, you know.

[Returns to the forced cheerfulness.]

As for me, I suppose you could say, prodded by my father, I've kept up my comic singing for the public these fifty-odd years!

My father also inspired my madness for walking up and down the countryside. The two of us would go off together, you know, when I was very young to be going such long distances.

It was on one such country walk that we came down this very road, and my father showed me this very same stout Georgian dwelling. I vividly remember staring at the bow windows and the small turret.

It was at that moment that he told me—my impecunious, extravagant, ever ill-starred father told me—that if I were to work very hard, I might come to live in this place some day.

And so I did. And so I have.

[Proudly.]

I made Wilkins Micawber out of my poor father—and much of Mr. Dorrit, along with parts of several other of my characters. But my father was a most memorable character himself.

[Very sober.]

I was with him when he died.

[Pause.]

I bought this place five years to the month after he died. Funny how the period of five years is repeating itself in my thoughts today. I had a special plaque made soon afterwards. You see it in the hall there, just be the door.

[Dickens narrating grandly in a voice suggestive of a Shakespearean prologue.]

"This house, Gads Hill Place, stands on the summit of Shakespeare's Gads Hill, ever memorable for its association with Sir John Falstaff in his noble fancy."

[Dickens as the irrepressible Falstaff.]

"My lads, my lads—tomorrow morning by four o'clock, early at Gads Hill, there are pilgrims going to Canterbury with rich offerings, and traders riding to London with fat purses. I have vizards for you all. You have horses for yourselves."

[A Falstaffian laugh punctuates the reading of the plaque.]

Yes, I did work hard, from the very beginning, when I was only a boy pasting labels on bottles of boot blacking while my father and the rest of the family languished in the Marshalsea Prison. And I worked hard as a Parliamentary reporter. And I worked doubly hard as a young author, and as a publisher and editor and general do-gooder.

And it all did result in my coming to live in this place. But, as you can see, none of that has soothed or satisfied me.

I have always been looking for something I have not found in life, but may possibly come to in a few thousand years hence, in some other part of some other system, God knows.

Once or twice, perhaps, I thought I had chanced on it—that something I had not found in life.

When I was a mere boy, but doing a man's work, I fell in love most terribly. At one point, I was practically the embodiment of the old enchanter whose familiars tore him to pieces. I revealed all of this in *David Copperfield*, without actually admitting how much of it was true. I wearied of rest, and had no satisfaction but in fatigue.

Realities and idealities were always comparing themselves before me, and I remember disliking the realities—except when they were unattainable. When they were unattainable, I liked them above all things!

I wished I had been born in the days of ogres and dragon-guarded castles. I wished that an ogre with seven heads and no particular evidence of brains in the whole of them had taken the princess whom I adored—you can have no idea how intensely I adored her—to his stronghold on the top of a high series of mountains, and there tied her up by the hair.

Nothing would have suited me so well, during much of that time, as climbing up after her, sword in hand, and either winning her, or being killed!

There's a frame of mind for you in the nineteenth century!

All this comes of being born into a utilitarian age, an age of railway disasters, and into a nation without romance—or with the wrong kind.

And it comes also of having made a miserable mistake when I was still very young, after I had lost any chance of winning the hand of that particular princess, ogres or not.

I refer now to my unfortunate marriage. The wretched consequences which might naturally have been expected from it, have resulted in it. That is all.

[Bitter, but instructive.]

Mistakes breed mistakes, and misunderstandings breed misunderstandings. And, in my case, all of it gets into the newspapers.

You may have heard rumours about my supposed relations with a young lady, Miss Ternan, the actress. I candidly admit I felt a great deal toward her—and still do.

[Self-righteous, tending toward disgusted.]

You must believe me when I say that I was perfectly innocent in my purchase of a bracelet for Ellen—Miss Ternan, that is. But the jeweler made the dreadful mistake of sending it to Tavistock House, where it fell into Kate's hands.

It was just one of those unfortunate developments that led to innocent people being spoken about—and written about—mercilously.

I had to put a stop to it, so I published that statement:

[Dickens as himself, angry, indignant, and yet dignified.]

"All the lately whispered rumours are abominably false, and whosoever repeats one of them after this denial will lie as willfully and foully as it is possible for any false witness to lie before heaven and earth."

Hmmmmph.

I had thought that statement would put a stop to all that, but of course it didn't—and, unfortunately, I lost some friends over it. Thackeray, for one, sad to say.

Soon, they will be saying the girl is pregnant. All this, simply because I have had to take great pains to protect her under the circumstances.

So, you see, there's no use speaking of such things. If you want to believe the worst, you will, despite anything I might say to you.

[Increasingly exasperated, and moving toward anger.]

No man but a fool was ever talked out of his own opinion and into your state of mind. Arguments are only cannonballs fired into a sandbank—or water poured into a sieve—a sheer waste of time and trouble.

I won't argue with a man; it is going down on all-fours to an obstinate dog.

In emphatic cases, the only argument is a punch in the head. That's a stunner!

[Firm, becoming calmer, determined.]

In fact, what I have always fallen back on in times of trouble is the one serviceable, safe, certain, remunerative attainable quality in any activity: the quality of attention.

My own invention, or imagination, such as it is, would never have served me as it has, but for the simple habit—excluding all distractions of every kind—of commonplace, humble, patient, daily, toiling, drudging attention.

Speaking of which, I must be attending to *Drood*.

[*Drood* narrator's voice, peaceful.]

"A brilliant morning shines on the old city . . . ."

[Suddenly agitated.]

That reminds me of something. What is it? Yes, I've called this "The Dawn Again." The Dawn. That's it!

[Sikes and Nancy narrator, suspenseful and sinister; melodramatic.]

"The bright sun burst upon the crowded city in clear and radiant glory. Through costly-colored glass and paper-mended window, through cathedral dome and rotten crevice, it shed its equal ray."

[Frightening intensity now.]

"It lighted up the rooms where the murdered woman lay. It did. The murderer tried to shut it out, but it would stream in. If the sight had been a ghastly one in the dull morning, what was it, now, in all that brilliant light!!!"

[Dickens' own marginal note at this point in his Reading Copy: "Terror to the End."]

"The Housebreaker had not moved all night; he had been afraid to stir. There had once been a moan and a motion of the hand; and with terror added to rage, he had struck and struck again."

"Once he threw a rug over it; but it was worse to fancy the eyes, and imagine them moving toward him, than to see them glaring upward, as if watching the reflection of the pool of gore that quivered and danced in the sunlight on the ceiling."

"He had plucked the rug off again. And there was the body—mere flesh and blood, no more—but such flesh, and so much blood!!!"

[CD in his own astonished, desperate voice.]

Great God! The greatest mystery in all the earth, to me, is how or why the world was tolerated by its Creator through the good old times, and wasn't dashed to fragments.

Five years ago tomorrow, I was very nearly dashed to fragments myself. And dear Ellen, too God bless her!

I beg your pardon. Where was I? Thank God, my doctors are all far away.

[Resuming the terror.]

"He struck a light, kindled a fire, and thrust the club into it. There was hair upon the end, which shrunk into a light cinder, and whirled up the chimney."

"Even that frightened him; but he held the weapon until it broke, and then piled it on the coals to burn away, and smoulder into ashes."

"He washed himself, and rubbed his clothes; there were spots upon them that would not be removed, but he cut the pieces out and burnt them."

"How those stains were dispersed about the room! The very feet of his dog were bloody!!!!"

[CD, gasping, in his own voice, short of breath.]

If I am not careful, the Housebreaker will rob me of my last bit of writing! He may yet drive me out of my mind. Or worse still, murder me. I must think only of *Drood* now. Attention, that's it.

[Reading what he has recently written, resignedly.]

"The cold stone tombs of centuries grow warm, and flecks of brightness dart into the sternest marble corners of the building, fluttering there like wings . . . ."

[Back to "The Murder," in spite of himself, and projecting the increasing panic and horror of The Housebreaker, trying to escape from the pursuing police and public.]

"The Housebreaker set his foot against the stack of chimneys, fastened one end of the rope firmly around it, and with the other made a strong running noose by the aid of his hands and teeth."

"With the cord running round his back, he could let himself down within a less distance of the ground than his own height, and had his knife ready in his hand to cut the cord, and drop."

"At the instant he brought the loop over his head before slipping it beneath his armpits, looking behind him on the roof he threw up his arms and yelled, 'The eyes again!'"

"Staggering as if struck by lightning, he lost his balance and tumbled over the parapet. The noose was at his neck; it ran up with his weight; tight as a bowstring, and swift as the arrow it speeds."

"He fell five-and-thirty feet, and hung with his open knife clenched in his stiffening hand!!!"

"The dog, which had lain concealed 'til now, ran backwards and forwards on the parapet with a dismal howl, and, collecting himself for a spring, jumped for the dead man's shoulders."

"Missing his aim, he fell into the ditch, turning over as he went, and striking against a stone, dashed out his brains!!"

[Gasps, collects himself, resumes his own exhausted voice.]

These violent delights have violent ends. Perhaps I will attempt no more of *Drood* just now.

If you will excuse me, I believe I shall have a cigar in my conservatory. It's brand new—a brilliant success, but, as all my successes have proven to be, an expensive one. Positively the last improvement.

CODA

Dickens suffered a stroke at dinner. He remained unconscious until his death the following afternoon. Against his expressed wishes, his body was taken by a special train from Gads Hill to London, where it was placed in Westminster Abbey for public viewing on the fourteenth of June. The grave remained open for three days, to permit thousands upon thousands of members of his devoted public to pay their last respects.